Remove Malware, Spyware and Viruses From Your PC

Hugh Mendoza

Copyright © Book Skim Publishing

Get This As a FREE Audiobook via Amazon's Audible.com

Visit: Bookskim.com/free

Chapter 1
What is Spyware?

It is normal to see pop-up ads while surfing the net, right? What a lot of people don't realize is that those ads could have made their way onto their computers through spyware. By the time that you figure out what is behind the ads, the spyware pop-ups may have gotten so bad that your only choice is to completely reconfigure your computer and just hope that the pop-ups don't come back. And, if your only mechanism to fight against the spyware is hope, the pop-up ads will return.

What is Spyware Exactly?

Spyware is a type of software which gets onto your computer and is generally used to gather your personal information and then send advertisements to you, normally in the form of a pop-up ad. Spyware software can also change your computer configuration as well as many other potentially harmful things. Even though the term spyware may suggest that the software is simply monitoring action in a secretive way, the purpose of spyware usually goes well beyond this. The party responsible for creating and distributing the spyware are often profiting greatly through targeted advertising or selling off your personal information.

When spyware software is on a computer, it generally is hidden from the user. In 2005, a study carried out by AOL and the National Cyber-Security Alliance showed that 61% of user's computers were infected with spyware. Of all of these users, 92% of them were not aware that their computers were even infected. 91% of the users claimed that they had not granted permission for the spyware software to be installed. Since then, spyware has become increasingly sophisticated and is often impossible to detect on a user's computer. Even worse, once detected, some spyware is impossible to remove.

Difference between Spyware and Adware

The terms spyware and adware are often used interchangeably. Both of these terms are used to describe software which can display advertisements. However, there is one major difference between these two: spyware gets onto the user's computer through illicit means.

With adware, the user agrees to have the adware program installed in exchange for something else. For example, the program Eudora will allow users access to shareware for free but they must agree to receive advertisements. The key word here is "agree." Adware will not attempt to mislead users and is offered in exchange for a service.

An example of adware includes the file sharing program Eudora. Rather than asking users to pay a registration fee, it asks them to agree to receive advertisements. On the other hand, Gator software is a type of spyware. When users visit certain websites, spyware is installed on the users' computer through some sort of deceptive manner. The company behind Gator as well as the website where the spyware was installed will both receive revenue.

Chapter 2
How is Spyware different from Viruses &Worms?

Today, there are an incalculable number of "health" problems that a computer can be at risk for. Generally, these risks can be broken down into spyware, viruses and worms. It is easy to confuse these different types of computer problems because they have many similarities.

Spyware, viruses and worms all get onto a user's computer with permission or by using deceptive means. Once on the computer, they cause harm to the computer and impair functions. Spyware, viruses and worms are all designed to be difficult, if not impossible, to detect. They often are designed in a certain way that prohibits them from being removed in normal manners. Recently, there have been many viruses and worms which have been, as spyware is, created for profit.

Compared to viruses and worms, spyware is a relatively new problem. Viruses have been around since the 1980s and worms almost as long. Spyware didn't become a major issue until 2000.

The major difference between spyware and viruses and worms is that spyware doesn't seek to replicate once on your computer. It also doesn't seek to infect other computers. Both viruses and worms, on the other hand, actively replicate themselves and can spread to other computers through means such as email.

Another big difference between spyware, viruses and worms is objective. Spyware is always used for some form of monetary gain such as through advertisements. Modern viruses and worms can also be used for monetary gain. However, viruses and worms are often created in an attempt to gain fame.

Some virus and worm creators have claimed their motivation was to show how far virus creation has advanced. Other creators desire to "outdo" the creators of anti-virus and anti-worm software.

As in the case with the Bagel and Netsky viruses, the creators of the viruses wanted to outdo each other.

Additionally, viruses and worms are often created specifically to do damage to a computer through a type of web espionage. An example of this is the Conflicker worm which spread in 2008. It made its way into the defense systems of France and Britain as well as about 15 million computers around the world and creating severe damage to the computers' health. Spyware, however, does not want to cause severe damage to the computer. That is because it relies on the computer's health in order to send advertisements to users.

Is there a Spy-Vir-Orm Hybrid?

It is getting increasingly difficult to distinguish between spyware, viruses and worms. As all three of these computer health issues become increasingly sophisticated, they have taken on properties of one another and often rely upon one another for functioning.

There are many instances when spyware is spread through a virus or visa versa. There are also many instances of spyware, worms or viruses creating openings for other types of harm to enter a user's computer. Because of this crossover between the spyware, viruses and worms, it is important that countermeasures are taken against all forms of computer infections.

Chapter 3
Can I Just Ignore Spyware?

Because spyware doesn't progressively destroy a computer's functioning like viruses and worms do, it may be possible to simply ignore the fact that your computer is infected. Many people figure that it is better to simply keep closing all those annoying pop-up ads rather than bother with antispyware software, some of which can be very expensive. Ignoring the fact you have spyware is a temporary solution but it can end up costing you in the long run.

Much of the spyware software now will disable firewalls, disable anti-virus software, and change browser security settings to low. This allows for further infection of your computer by other spyware software or viruses and worms. At first, you may just have a few pop-up ads. Later, this may progress to the point where the pop-ups come faster than you can click to close them or your computer is getting destroyed by a cocktail of viruses as though your computer has an immune deficiency disease.

Spyware software makers were aware that this change in security settings would allow other spyware to get into the computer. Because spyware companies are in competition against each other, some spyware actually destroys other spyware which is on your computer. This also keeps users from taking action against spyware because the problem never seemingly gets too bad. The spyware maker Avenue Media actually sued one of its competitors called Direct Revenue because the company disabled its spyware. The two companies settled the dispute by agreeing not to disable each other's products.

Aside from the lowered security settings that many spyware programs create, you may have gotten a virus or worm with your spyware in a bundled package. This cocktail of computer infections can do serious and even irreversible damage. Even if you don't have an additional problem other than spyware, you can never be sure exactly what the spyware is doing and what information of yours it is accessing – such as your credit card numbers.

By ignoring the threat of spyware, you are setting up your computer for a potential disaster. Antispyware programs can be very expensive however, if you take the time to educate yourself, there are plenty of free antispyware programs. Even if you opt for the paid versions, it is better to spend that money now than to pay to have your computer completely reconfigured in the future after the spyware problem gets out of control.

Chapter 4
What Damage Can Spyware Do?

Bombards You with Advertisements

Spyware is known for displaying advertisements, usually in the form of pop-ups. Each spyware software program works a bit differently with its advertising. Some display ads every couple of minutes, for example, while others will display every time you open a new browser window. The newest sure exactly what the spyware is doing and what information of yours it is accessing – such as your credit card numbers.

By ignoring the threat of spyware, you are setting up your computer for a potential disaster. Antispyware programs can be very expensive however, if you take the time to educate yourself, there are plenty of free antispyware programs. Even if you opt for the paid versions, it is better to spend that money now than to pay to have your computer completely reconfigured in the future after the spyware problem gets out of control.

Chapter 4
What Damage Can Spyware Do?

Bombards You with Advertisements

Spyware is known for displaying advertisements, usually in the form of pop-ups. Each spyware software program works a bit differently with its advertising. Some display ads every couple of minutes, for example, while others will display every time you open a new browser window. The newest trend amongst spyware is to track what the user is doing online. Then, this information is relayed so specific, targeted ads are displayed. For people vulnerable to advertising, these targeted ads can be a great threat.

These pop-up ads can be a great nuisance. Also, pornography pop-up ads are a very common issue with spyware and they are considered particularly heinous because children could be exposed to the porn ads.

Another way in which spyware may advertise is to take over the banner ads. Instead of seeing the advertisement which the site's creator put up, the viewer sees a spyware ad instead. Because many websites are funded by ads, the spyware is stealing profit from the website owner as well as annoying the viewer with the banner ad.

Slower Computer

When a computer is infected with spyware, it must process the spyware applications. All of the tasks that spyware can do from displaying pop-up ads to tracking users are very demanding on a computer's system. This results in the computer going slower and sometimes drastically slower. If the spyware relayed so specific, targeted ads are displayed. For people vulnerable to advertising, these targeted ads can be a great threat.

These pop-up ads can be a great nuisance. Also, pornography pop-up ads are a very common issue with spyware and they are considered particularly heinous because children could be exposed to the porn ads.

Another way in which spyware may advertise is to take over the banner ads. Instead of seeing the advertisement which the site's creator put up, the viewer sees a spyware ad instead. Because many websites are funded by ads, the spyware is stealing profit from the website owner as well as annoying the viewer with the banner ad.

Slower Computer

When a computer is infected with spyware, it must process the spyware applications. All of the tasks that spyware can do from displaying pop-up ads to tracking users are very demanding on a computer's system. This results in the computer going slower and sometimes drastically slower. If the spyware problem gets out of hand, it is possible for the computer to crash because it can't handle all of the applications that are being requested from it.

Identity Theft and Fraud

True to its name, there are new versions of spyware which can literally spy on the user. The spyware will take pictures of the websites that a user visits and then relay the pictures back to the spyware source. Since website pages can contain banking information and other personal information, spyware can lead to identity theft. These types of spyware are rare but they still exist.

With dial-up internet access, there is also the risk of wire fraud. This occurs when spyware resets a modem to dial up numbers at a premium rate rather than the usually number for the ISP. This results in large phone bills for the user.

Changing Settings

One of the common things that spyware does is to change a computer's configurations. Generally, the web browser homepage will be changed along with the search engine.

Spyware can also change security levels and even prevent a user from installing or running antivirus or antispyware programs. Once these changes have been made by the spyware, it is usually very difficult to get the settings back to normal.

Stealware

For affiliates selling products online, spyware can pose risk for a different type of fraud. When a sale is made through an affiliate, the spyware will fill in the affiliate's tag with the tag of the spyware operator. Instead of the legitimate affiliate getting paid for the sale, the spyware operate benefits instead. In this case, only the spyware operate is benefiting from the illicit software. The New York Times dubbed this type of affiliate fraud "stealware."

Virtual Spying

Spyware has been used to virtually spy on people in several cases. In some cases, spyware was put onto a computer so that the activity of the user could be monitored. The software Loverspy is an example of this type of spyware which was marketed towards people suspecting that their spouse/partner was infidel. There are also instances when spyware was used to turn on webcams so the spyware operator could spy on the user. Depending on the areas where it is used, this type of spyware monitoring may be illegal, even if used by a spouse.

Chapter 5
How does Spyware Get onto Your Computer?

You Install It

In most cases, spyware gets onto your computer because you have installed it unknowingly. This is how it works: when you find some sort of free program or file online, you download it and it comes bundled together with spyware. This is also the case with shareware. For spyware creators like Claria, which is the largest spyware company, this method of spyware transmission is very profitable. Claria had revenues of $35 million just last year.

Spyware as a profitable business really began to surge when free internet applications infidel. There are also instances when spyware was used to turn on webcams so the spyware operator could spy on the user. Depending on the areas where it is used, this type of spyware monitoring may be illegal, even if used by a spouse.

Chapter 5
How does Spyware Get onto Your Computer?

You Install It

In most cases, spyware gets onto your computer because you have installed it unknowingly. This is how it works: when you find some sort of free program or file online, you download it and it comes bundled together with spyware. This is also the case with shareware. For spyware creators like Claria, which is the largest spyware company, this method of spyware transmission is very profitable. Claria had revenues of $35 million just last year.

Spyware as a profitable business really began to surge when free internet applications became available online. Since applications such as Web browser, email, and instant messaging were free, it didn't take long before users expected free software as well. Software makers were having a hard time selling software for even low prices and they had trouble battling against illegal file sharing as well. Instead of trying to increase sales, the software makers decided to offer free software but include spyware bundled with it.

A spyware company will pay a software company for every time the software is installed. Then, the spyware uses targeted ads on the user. When a user clicks on the ad or makes a purchase through the ad, the spyware company profits.

An example of this is the free file sharing application Kazaa which comes bundled with spyware from the company Claria. Kazaa gets paid by Claria every time its program is installed. Then, the Claria spyware creates targeted pop-up ads for users and profits each time one of those ads is clicked on. If you visit the Dish Network homepage, a pop-up ad for DirecTV will appear.

This method of spyware distribution occurs with all sorts of free downloads including software and file sharing. Often, the terms and conditions for downloading a free application will mention that spyware is included with the download. However, not many people take the time to read through the terms and conditions. It is also common for the information about spyware to be deceptively hidden in a very long and confusing terms and conditions statement. The downloader simply clicks "Accept" and gets the spyware.

Fake Windows Security Boxes

To start downloading spyware, sometimes all it takes is a click of a link. One of the most common ways that spyware makers get users to click on their links is by disguising them as Windows security boxes.

The boxes look just like a normal Windows security box. However, when you click on them, the link causes your security settings to change and spyware to be installed on your computer without your knowledge. For example, a box might read, "Optimize your software and file sharing. Often, the terms and conditions for downloading a free application will mention that spyware is included with the download. However, not many people take the time to read through the terms and conditions. It is also common for the information about spyware to be deceptively hidden in a very long and confusing terms and conditions statement. The downloader simply clicks "Accept" and gets the spyware.

Fake Windows Security Boxes

To start downloading spyware, sometimes all it takes is a click of a link. One of the most common ways that spyware makers get users to click on their links is by disguising them as Windows security boxes.

The boxes look just like a normal Windows security box. However, when you click on them, the link causes your security settings to change and spyware to be installed on your computer without your knowledge. For example, a box might read, "Optimize your internet access." Even if you hit the "No" button, you will still trigger the spyware.

Security Holes

If you do not have high security on your computer, you run the risk of spyware finding its way inside. Some of the newer spyware programs have even learned to find their way through holes in firewall and antispyware software. Spyware is often distributed with a virus. First, a virus is sent to a computer. Instead of replicating and possibly destroying a computer's system like a normal virus, its job is instead to create a hole for the spyware to enter.

There are several other illicit ways in which spyware can enter a computer. For example, there are spyware programs which are spread through emails. Even if the email gets tagged as potentially dangerous and the user doesn't read it, the spyware can still be spread just by having it displayed in a preview pane.

Chapter 6
How to Prevent Spyware

Because there are so many different ways for spyware to enter a computer, it is almost impossible to avoid infection. Avoiding certain activities, such as downloading, can reduce the risk but there are still many ways for spyware to enter. That is why preventative and real-time counteractive measures need to be taken.

The first step to preventing spyware infections (and re-infections after spyware is removed) is to educate yourself. By understanding why spyware exists, you can start to identify possible threats while you are online. So, if you skipped the first five chapters of this eBook, now would be a good time to go back and read them before continuing on.

Research Before You Download

Even though downloading any sort of free file or software is one of the biggest risks when it comes to getting spyware or other computer infections, most people are not going to stop downloading. There are simply too many desirable free programs and files out there.

However, you can greatly reduce the risk of an infection by researching the freebie first.

Whenever downloading free software, type its name into a reputable search engine along with the word spyware. Chances are, if that program comes bundled with spyware, you won't be the first to get it. If you type in "Kazaa spyware" into Google, for example, the first several pages of results all mention the infamous spyware as well as how to remove it.

Change Your Settings

Some of the preventative steps against spyware are very simple to take. For example, you can use Mozilla Firefox instead of Microsoft's browsers which have several security holes which are easy for spyware programs to enter through. Also, switching to a Mac or Linux operating system will greatly reduce your risk of various computer infections because most are targeted at Windows. However, this is not such an easy change to make.

If working on Windows Explorer, you will want to install Windows XP Service Pack 2. This service pack solves many of the security holes in Internet Explorer and it also has a built-in pop-up blocker. There are also features like the add-on manager which will allow you monitor which programs are running with Internet Explorer. You can download Windows XP Service Pack 2 here:

http://www.microsoft.com/windowsxp/sp2/default.mspx

You will also want to change your Security Zone settings on Internet Explorer to block harmful sites. The settings have the options of listing sites as Trusted, Restricted, Local Internet, or Internet. If you list a site as restricted, you are still able to visit that site but the security settings will prevent the site from harming your computer. Some antispyware tools like Spyware Blaster and Spybot Search and Destroy will add automatically add harmful sites to the restricted setting.

This service pack solves many of the security holes in Internet Explorer and it also has a built-in pop-up blocker. There are also features like the add-on manager which will allow you monitor which programs are running with Internet Explorer. You can download Windows XP Service Pack 2 here:

http://www.microsoft.com/windowsxp/sp2/default.mspx

You will also want to change your Security Zone settings on Internet Explorer to block harmful sites. The settings have the options of listing sites as Trusted, Restricted, Local Internet, or Internet. If you list a site as restricted, you are still able to visit that site but the security settings will prevent the site from harming your computer. Some antispyware tools like Spyware Blaster and Spybot Search and Destroy will add automatically add harmful sites to the restricted setting.

If your computer internet is connected to a dial-up modem, you will want to unplug the modem when you aren't using it. This will prevent spyware from committing dial fraud by calling premium numbers.

Chapter 7
What is Antispyware & How Does it Work?

There are a few different types of antispyware software. The most common type will run a scan of your computer and determine if there are any spyware programs there. You can usually choose how often the scan will be done such as on a daily or weekly basis. Generally, these are the areas which get checked in a spyware scan:

Window's registry

Operating system files

Files which have been installed through programs

 Some antispyware scanning software will allow you to do "smart scans" where only the computer files which are commonly infected with spyware will be scanned. This type of scan is much faster than a full scan though it is not as accurate.

If spyware software is detected on your computer, there are antispyware software programs which will attempt to delete them. There are also antispyware software programs which will work in real time to block any attempts to infect your computer as they happen.

The real time antispyware blockers work in a few different ways. Some of them have mass lists of known spyware software which they will automatically block. Others will locate any suspicious program which is attempting to download on your computer. The antispyware blocker will not automatically block the download. Rather, it will send the user an alert. Then the user can make a choice as to whether to allow or deny the download.

There is also antispyware software which will intercept programs that attempt to install startup items or change browser settings. The best antispyware protection comes

If spyware software is detected on your computer, there are antispyware software programs which will attempt to delete them. There are also antispyware software programs which will work in real time to block any attempts to infect your computer as they happen.

The real time antispyware blockers work in a few different ways. Some of them have mass lists of known spyware software which they will automatically block. Others will locate any suspicious program which is attempting to download on your computer. The antispyware blocker will not automatically block the download. Rather, it will send the user an alert. Then the user can make a choice as to whether to allow or deny the download.

There is also antispyware software which will intercept programs that attempt to install startup items or change browser settings. The best antispyware protection comes

from having all three of these elements: detection through scanning, spyware removal, and real time protection.

Many computer security software programs contain antispyware programs. However, do not assume that they do. It is important that you are getting full coverage against spyware and many of the computer security software programs only fight against viruses and worms.

Chapter 8
Can I Use "All-Around" Computer Security Software?

When a virus enters a computer, it can do a lot of damage, especially in terms of overall health. Once the "immune system" of a computer has been harmed by a virus, it becomes much easier for other forms of malware to enter the system. Some viruses are even specifically designed to penetrate a computer's security simply to make a hole for spyware to enter. Because of these factors, it is important that your computer also have antivirus in addition to antispyware software.

Many people have the mistaken belief that their antivirus or computer security software contains antispyware software as well.

However, this is often not the case. Many antivirus makers are reluctant to include antispyware at all. That is because they worry that their antispyware could block a legitimate software or advertising program and then they would be subject to a lawsuit.

Even when antispyware is included with an antivirus, it is generally not enough protection. An article from Wired magazine from June 25th, 2004 explored this problem. A test was performed by purposely attempting to infect a computer with spyware while running antivirus software which also had antispyware capabilities:

"All the antivirus programs popped up a warning when they detected an attempt to install spyware. In most cases, all the antivirus programs successfully deleted the spyware they spotted after it was installed, but none could fully repair the damage -- they were unable to remove toolbars installed by some of the spyware, or restore registry settings.

In some cases, with more virulent pieces of spyware, Symantec, McAfee and Trend Micro's antivirus applications were unable to antivirus makers are reluctant to include antispyware at all. That is because they worry that their antispyware could block a legitimate software or advertising program and then they would be subject to a lawsuit.

Even when antispyware is included with an antivirus, it is generally not enough protection. An article from Wired magazine from June 25th, 2004 explored this problem. A test was performed by purposely attempting to infect a computer with spyware while running antivirus software which also had antispyware capabilities:

"All the antivirus programs popped up a warning when they detected an attempt to install spyware. In most cases, all the antivirus programs successfully deleted the spyware they spotted after it was installed, but none could fully repair the damage -- they were unable to remove toolbars installed by some of the spyware, or restore registry settings.

In some cases, with more virulent pieces of spyware, Symantec, McAfee and Trend Micro's antivirus applications were unable to fully purge the software from the infected machine. Although the system was reported as clean, the spyware reactivated after a reboot."

Because the awareness and risks of spyware have increased since the Wired article, there have been some major improvements in the development of all-around computer protection. However, it is still best to have separate antivirus software to accompany your antispyware software.

Chapter 9
Free Antispyware Software

One of the reasons that spyware is spread so quickly is because of all the free downloads which have spyware software bundled in with them. Obviously, many people are not willing to pay for software- especially antispyware software. Luckily, there is now a lot of free antispyware software available.

One of the ways to get free antispyware software is simply to download it from the internet. However, it is very common that the free antispyware software actually comes with spyware bundled in with it. You can read the next chapter to find out about this risk. Here is a list of some of the best antispyware software programs available for free online.

Windows Defender: Before any software can be installed, it has to pass a Windows Genuine Advantage test. This antispyware software works in real time. It takes up little running space and can be put on a schedule for scanning a computer system. However, it is not the best choice of software for stopping all spyware.

Spybot Search & Destroy: This is one of the most well-known antispyware software programs. It has been around since 2000 and is regularly updated. It has an immunization feature which will add malicious sites to your Restricted Sites list to protect you in case your computer is hijacked and taken to a harmful site.

Ad-Aware: Ad-Aware is another one of the most popular free antispyware software. It can be downloaded for free. However, there is also a commercial version of Ad-Aware which offers even higher levels of protection. It also includes antivirus.

AVG Anti-Spyware Free Edition: AVG is popular became popular as antivirus software and now has created antispyware software as well. There is a commercial and a free version available. AVG is one of strongest in terms of overall computer protection. However, like all free antispyware software, it does not contain a built-in firewall.

Avast! antivirus Home Edition: This software is a combination of antivirus, antispyware and anti-rootkit. It is made for Windows and is free for home use.

Panda Cloud Antivirus: This program also includes antispyware

Microsoft Malicious Software Removal Tool: Called MSRT for shot, this software is available for free so long as your Windows is genuine. There are free monthly updates of

MSRT available for users on the first Tuesday of each month.

Comodo Internet Security: The Comodo company makes several software programs including antispyware, antivirus, and a firewall. You can download each of these separately for maximum protection. There is also a paid version called Comodo Internet Security Pro. Comodo is one of the strongest when it comes to battling computer infections. However, the software may be a bit difficult for beginners to operate and the free version doesn't have any customer support.

Spyware Blaster: This software does not remove spyware infections. Its goal is to prevent spyware infection and has a list of thousands of malicious sites which can be added to your Restricted Sites list. It also has a feature which will allow you to lock your Internet Explorer homepage so it can't be altered.

SuperAntiSpyware: If you already have a spyware infection, this software has been reported as effective in removing the spyware.

HijackThis: This freeware utility works a bit differently than most spyware removal tools because it doesn't just perform a simple scan based on a list of spyware. Instead, it scans the computer and looks for all suspicious items. Then, HijackThis will ask the user what to do with those items. Users should be very careful while using HijackThis to not delete any useful or essential items.

Removal Restrictions Tool: Also known as RRT, this tool is used to restore permissions in situations where spyware has locked users from the Control Panel, Task Manager or Regedit.

There are a lot more free antispyware programs available with new ones constantly becoming available. However, it is important to note that many of these are not completely effective in preventing or removing spyware. Usually, they each have a few loopholes which spyware makers are aware of and exploit.

One way to get around the loopholes is to use multiple free antispyware software programs at once. What one program misses will generally be picked up by another program.

The only real downside to this method is that using multiple antispyware programs can make your computer run slower.

Also, it needs to be pointed out that many of the free antispyware which is advertised online is actually rogue antispyware. This software actually contains spyware which will infect your computer.

Chapter 10
Rogue Antispyware Software

You need to be really careful when choosing antispyware to install. There are an increasing number of fake antispyware software programs out there and they all appear legitimate at first.

The way that antispyware usually strikes is with a pop-up window that reads something like, "Your Computer is Infected!" In one scenario, the user would then be guided through a step-by-step process for purchasing the antispyware software and have all of the "alleged" spyware and viruses cleaned. In this situation, the user is tricked out of money and using multiple antispyware programs can make your computer run slower.

Also, it needs to be pointed out that many of the free antispyware which is advertised online is actually rogue antispyware. This software actually contains spyware which will infect your computer.

Chapter 10
Rogue Antispyware Software

You need to be really careful when choosing antispyware to install. There are an increasing number of fake antispyware software programs out there and they all appear legitimate at first.

The way that antispyware usually strikes is with a pop-up window that reads something like, "Your Computer is Infected!" In one scenario, the user would then be guided through a step-by-step process for purchasing the antispyware software and have all of the "alleged" spyware and viruses cleaned. In this situation, the user is tricked out of money and may also have his/her credit card information stolen.

In another scenario, users are tricked into downloading software which is completely free. Instead of getting free antispyware, this software actually contains spyware.

Even though these rogue antispyware software programs look just like legitimate software at first, they are pretty easy to detect.

How to Detect Fake Antispyware

There are many sites out there which give lists of legitimate and rogue antispyware software. While this can be a surefire way to see if a program is legit, this method isn't recommended for a few reasons. First of all, the amount of legit and fake software is changing all the time. It is hard to know if the list you are looking at is updated or not. Also, you may not know for sure if the list is even legit. Plus, looking at a list means that you have to go through a huge amount of software names. Since many of the fake antispyware software have names which mirror legitimate software, it can be confusing to distinguish the two.

The quickest and easiest way to determine if software is legit or not is by simply typing its name into a reputable search engine. The internet community is generally pretty quick to respond whenever new spyware software hits. The results you get from the search will be fairly simple to interpret.

For example, if you type into Google's search engine "Windows Care Tool," which is rogue internet security software, you get results like this:

"Windows Care Tool - how to remove"

http://www.2-viruses.com/remove-windows-care-tool

9 Feb 2011 ... Windows Care Tool is a malicious program that was designed for the one big purpose which is to rip users off. As any other representative ...

www.2-viruses.com/remove-windows-care-tool

Remove Windows Care Tool (Uninstall Guide)

http://www.bleepingcomputer.com/virus-removal/remove-windows-care-tool

9 Feb 2011 ... This page contains free removal instructions for Windows Care Tool.

Please use this guide to uninstall Windows Care Tool and any associated ... www.bleepingcomputer.com/virus-removal/remove-windows-care-tool

Remove Windows Care Tool, removal instructions

http://www.2-spyware.com/remove-windows-care-tool.html

Windows Care Tool is a rogue anti-spyware program that displays fake security alerts and fake threats. This rogue is installed through the use of. www.2-spyware.com/remove-windows-care-tool.html

Obviously, Windows Care Tool is a rogue antispyware program because the internet would not be flooded with information on how to remove a useful program. Compare these results to the search results for "Spybot Search and Destroy," which is very useful antispyware software:

Spybot Search & Destroy

http://www.safer-networking.org/

Searches whole computer or just a certain file for malicious software commonly missed by anti-virus programs. Can be used to clean usage tracks.

www.safer-networking.org/

http://webcache.googleusercontent.com/search?q=cache:v8dD32xb7ewJ:www.safer-networking.org/+spybot+search+and+destroy&cd=1&hl=en&ct=clnk&client=firefox-a&source=www.google.com

http://www.google.com/search?hl=en&client=firefox-a&hs=rMI&rls=org.mozilla:en-US:official&q=related:www.safer-networking.org/+spybot+search+and+destroy&tbo=1&sa=X&ei=UgZTTZnUJZS_4gb1mIWqCA&sqi=2&ved=0CCkQHzAA

Spybot - Search & Destroy©® - The home of Spybot-S&D!

http://www.safer-networking.org/en/spybotsd/

Spybot - Search & Destroy detects and removes spyware, a relatively new kind ... www.safer-networking.org/en/spybotsd/ - http://webcache.googleusercontent.com/search?q=cache:GJm8xgQeysIJ:www.safer-networking.org/en/spybotsd/+spybot+search+and+destroy&cd=4&hl=en&ct=clnk&client=firefox-a&source=www.google.com

Show more results from safer-networking.org

http://www.google.com/search?q=Windows+Care+Tool&ie=utf-8&oe=utf-8&aq=t&rls=org.mozilla:en-US:official&client=firefox-a

Spybot - Search & Destroy - Free software downloads and software ...

http://download.cnet.com/Spybot-Search-amp-Destroy/3000-8022_4-10122137.htmlReview by CNET Staff - Nov 7, 2008

Spybot - Search & Destroy has been in the antispyware game for a long time offering features we've come to expect in the best apps in the category, ...

download.cnet.com/Spybot-
Search...Destroy/3000-8022_4-
10122137.html

http://webcache.googleusercontent.com/sear
ch?q=cache:om5JXqj4vx8J:download.cnet.co
m/Spybot-Search-amp-Destroy/3000-
8022_4-
10122137.html+spybot+search+and+destroy&
cd=5&hl=en&ct=clnk&client=firefox-
a&source=www.google.com

http://www.google.com/search?hl=en&client
=firefox-a&hs=rMI&rls=org.mozilla:en-
US:official&q=related:download.cnet.com/Sp
ybot-Search-amp-Destroy/3000-8022_4-
10122137.html+spybot+search+and+destroy&
tbo=1&sa=X&ei=UgZTTZnUJZS_4gb1mIWqC
A&sqi=2&ved=0CE8QHzAE

If you are still not sure about whether
software is legitimate or rogue, you can seek
out the software company's website. All
legitimate software should have a website
where you can find information about it.

It takes less than 30 seconds to type a
software name into a search engine. You

shouldn't skip this step because you could end up infected with spyware!

Chapter 11
Choosing Antispyware Software

There are a lot of antispyware software programs out there and all of them offer different levels of security. Before you antispyware software, you should at least take a few minutes to do some research and find out more about the software. You can easily get lists of the "best" antispyware software from blogs and websites. Then, use these lists for further investigation.

Here is what you should be finding out about the antispyware before downloading:

Who makes the antispyware: There are a lot of well-known companies which make antispyware, such as Microsoft. However, this doesn't mean that the big brand names are offering the best products. What is important is that the company has a good reputation for antispyware software. Some of the best companies have been around for a long time. Since they have been dealing with spyware issues for so long, they may be adept at fighting against the threat.

Are there any complaints about the company: Generally, you can easily uncover any complaints about an antispyware company simply by typing its name into a search engine. You may also want to try searching for the company's name followed by "complaints." If there are more negative comments than positive ones, you can be sure that there are major issues with that software program. To really be sure about the company's reputation, you can visit the website for the Better Business Bureau. There, you will find out if there are any unresolved complaints against the company.

How are its reviews: There are countless blogs and other websites which have reviews of antispyware software. Some of these are left by users while others

are by professionals in the field. To make sure that the reviews are accurate, you might want to check out reviews at sites like CNET.com which specialize in tech news.

Keep in mind that there is no one best antispyware software program. Rather, it matters which antispyware is best suited for your needs. Here are some other factors you should take into consideration:

How easy is the antispyware to use?

Does the antispyware come with customer support?

Will the antispyware slow down your computer?

Is the antispyware effective in prevention?

Is there real time prevention?

How effective is the software in spyware removal?

Do you need to update and, if so, are updates free?

What scanning options are there?

Does the antispyware include antivirus as well?

How much does the antispyware cost?

Almost all antispyware software today comes with a free trial period. It is highly recommended that you take advantage of this option in order to see how you like the antispyware before you decide to buy it.

Chapter 12
Do You Need to Update Antispyware?

Spyware is constantly becoming more sophisticated. As antispyware makers find ways to prevent the attacks, the spyware makers are finding holes in the systems through which they can send infections. The antispyware which was effective just one year ago will not likely be effective against the newer strains of spyware. Because of this, it is important that you regularly update your antispyware software.

How to Update Antispyware

If you have a paid subscription to an antispyware software program, then you will be able to update during the subscription period. Some companies will give you free updates for life if you buy their antispyware software. In these cases, the software will generally have an alert system

which will pop up a warning when you need to upgrade. Or, it may automatically do the update for you depending on what your settings are.

 With free antispyware software, you generally have to do the updating manually. That means remembering to periodically visit the site and download the newest version of the antispyware.

Antispyware with No Updating

There are a few antispyware software programs which don't require updating. These ones don't use the typical scanning method for finding spyware threats. Instead, they observe the history of the user's Window registry and browser. These specific parameters are monitored. Whenever anything attempts to change these parameters, the antispyware will alert the user. Then, the user decides what action to take.

While this type of antispyware is beneficial because it doesn't need updating, it has its drawbacks. Instead of offering suggestions about whether a program is harmful, the user must make that decision. This might require more time on the user's part rather than just allowing the antispyware software to make decisions.

Chapter 13
How to Get Rid of Spyware

If you have a spyware infection, then your best bet is to use antispyware software in order to find then remove the malicious software. If you already have antispyware software which didn't detect the attack, then you may need to use a different program in addition to this one.

Even though some antispyware defense systems are great, not one of them is impenetrable. Generally, the best method of preventing and getting rid of spyware is to use at least two antispyware programs. What one program misses will generally be picked up by the other program.

drawbacks. Instead of offering suggestions about whether a program is harmful, the user must make that decision. This might require more time on the user's part rather than just allowing the antispyware software to make decisions.

Chapter 13
How to Get Rid of Spyware

If you have a spyware infection, then your best bet is to use antispyware software in order to find then remove the malicious software. If you already have antispyware software which didn't detect the attack, then you may need to use a different program in addition to this one.

Even though some antispyware defense systems are great, not one of them is impenetrable. Generally, the best method of preventing and getting rid of spyware is to use at least two antispyware programs. What one program misses will generally be picked up by the other program.

The two free antispyware programs Ad Aware and Spybot Search & Destroy will almost always take care of a spyware problem when used together. For particularly heinous spyware attacks, you may need to use a commercial product. Spy Sweeper and Pest Patrol are both fairly good products.

If you still can't remove the spyware from your computer, then you will have to explore manual removal options.

Chapter 14
Spyware Removal in Safe Mode

If you can't remove a spyware infection with antispyware, then removal in safe mode is generally your next step. When Windows is run in Safe Mode, it is running using a minimal amount of drivers and services as well as isolating the computer from the internet.

The reason that safe mode is effective in spyware removal is because spyware is often hidden in the computer's memory. Antispyware generally focuses on the computer's hard disk rather than the memory. Thus, the spyware modules load while the antispyware attempts to clean it out.

used together. For particularly heinous spyware attacks, you may need to use a commercial product. Spy Sweeper and Pest Patrol are both fairly good products.

If you still can't remove the spyware from your computer, then you will have to explore manual removal options.

Chapter 14
Spyware Removal in Safe Mode

If you can't remove a spyware infection with antispyware, then removal in safe mode is generally your next step. When Windows is run in Safe Mode, it is running using a minimal amount of drivers and services as well as isolating the computer from the internet.

The reason that safe mode is effective in spyware removal is because spyware is often hidden in the computer's memory. Antispyware generally focuses on the computer's hard disk rather than the memory. Thus, the spyware modules load while the antispyware attempts to clean it out.

While in safe mode, the spyware in the memory won't be able to load and the antispyware will be able to effectively clean it out.

Running Antispyware in Safe Mode

Before you clean your computer in safe mode, you will need to boot your computer normally and download the most recent version of antispyware. If your computer isn't too badly infected to impede its functioning, you may want to download several different versions of antispyware.

After downloading the latest antispyware software, restart your computer. When the computer starts again, you will first see some information about equipment, hard drives, and so forth. Then, you will see a black screen with a white bar on the bottom which says "Starting Windows." When you see this, repeatedly tap the F8 button until an Advanced Options Menu appears.

While in safe mode, the spyware in the memory won't be able to load and the antispyware will be able to effectively clean it out.

Running Antispyware in Safe Mode

Before you clean your computer in safe mode, you will need to boot your computer normally and download the most recent version of antispyware. If your computer isn't too badly infected to impede its functioning, you may want to download several different versions of antispyware.

After downloading the latest antispyware software, restart your computer. When the computer starts again, you will first see some information about equipment, hard drives, and so forth. Then, you will see a black screen with a white bar on the bottom which says "Starting Windows." When you see this, repeatedly tap the F8 button until an Advanced Options Menu appears.

Use the arrow keys on your computer to select the Safe Mode option then press enter. The computer will then boot in safe mode. Once in safe mode, you can run your antispyware software and this will hopefully take care of the problem.

Using the System Configuration Method to Enter Safe Mode

If you can't get into Safe Mode with the F8 method, then you should try this method instead.

First, close any programs which are running. Then, click on the Start button and select Run. You should type msconfig in the Run field.

When you click OK, the System Configuration Utility will start.

Click on BOOT.INI. Then, in the area where it says Boot Options, put a checkmark in the /SAFEBOOT box. When you click Ok, you will be given an option to restart the computer. Click the Restart button. Your computer will restart in Safe Mode.

You will then be able to run the antispyware software in Safe Mode. When you finish, you will need to make sure that you follow the same steps as before but uncheck the /SAFEBOOT option. Then, under the General tab, you will need to select Normal Startup.

Chapter 15
Manual Removal of Spyware

There are many types of spyware which your antispyware will be able to detect but will not be able to remove. When this happens, your best bet is to remove the spyware manually. Be warned that this is often a very tedious process which takes careful examination of your computer system. Since spyware often exist with viruses, you may remove all of the spyware but miss a virus. Then, the spyware is able to quickly reappear through a hole that the virus made. However, if your antispyware system fails you, then this may be your best option.

Luckily, there are special tools for removing some of the most common spyware which are resistant to antispyware methods. One example of this tough strain of spyware is called Cool Web Search. The spyware will invade a user's system and then hijack the home page. Then, it will load the computer system with various Trojan viruses. Cool Web Search is very common but antispyware software makers have been having trouble combating it because there are countless forms of it.

For Cool Web Search, you can download a special tool called CWShredder. However, the strains of Cool Web Search spyware keep getting stronger and the new ones are resistant to CWShredder. For newer variations of the spyware, a utility called CoolWWWSearch Smart Killer will do the job. However, by the time you read this, this utility might already be useless against the newest strain of the spyware.

Manual Removal of Spyware Files and Entries

Unfortunately, not all spyware types have utility tools made specifically to combat them. Instead, you will have to destroy the spyware files and entries one by one. First, you must find out through your antispyware which type of spyware you have. Then, you can type in its name to a search engine and you should get lists of sites offering removal instructions or tools. There are a lot of great sites out there which will give you detailed descriptions of how to remove spyware software.

For example, the site www.spywareremove.com has great detailed instructions on just about every type of spyware. As new spyware is introduced, the site updates information so users can combat the spyware by manually deleting it.

Here is an example of what spyware removal instructions look like for a new type of spyware called MediaMotor:

Step 1: Use Windows Task Manager to Remove MediaMotor Processes Remove the "MediaMotor" processes files:

unstall.exe

switpa.exe

Switp_bund_ar14.exe

Switp_bund_ar14[1].exe

switp31[1].exe

tools. There are a lot of great sites out there which will give you detailed descriptions of how to remove spyware software.

For example, the site www.spywareremove.com has great detailed instructions on just about every type of spyware. As new spyware is introduced, the site updates information so users can combat the spyware by manually deleting it.

Here is an example of what spyware removal instructions look like for a new type of spyware called MediaMotor:

Step 1: Use Windows Task Manager to Remove MediaMotor Processes Remove the "MediaMotor" processes files:

unstall.exe

switpa.exe

Switp_bund_ar14.exe

Switp_bund_ar14[1].exe

switp31[1].exe

Step 2: Use Registry Editor to Remove MediaMotor Registry Values Locate and delete "MediaMotor" registry entries:

Microsoft\\Windows\CurrentVersion\Internet Settings\ZoneMap\Domains\mmohsix.com

Microsoft\\Windows\CurrentVersion\Internet Settings\ZoneMap\Domains\media-motor

EOCE16CB-741C-4B24-8D04-A817856E07F4

78A163D2-2358-464D-807B-0E2A078C7727

Switp

Step 3: Detect and Delete Other MediaMotor Files Remove the "MediaMotor"

processes files:

uninstall.exe

switpa.exe

Switp_bund_ar14.exe

Switp_bund_ar14[1].exe

switp31[1].exe

Step 4: View the MediaMotor Components with its MD5s

Remove the "MediaMotor" components:

File Name   adsetup_silent.1.53[1].e

File Size   11875

MD5   dc4a55fd8625e43e271188696431df

      xe   5   97

921ef076fb6745a727626d050ea4c7
tdopkpif.exe

36864

35 ec0590d49b53b51d24af35232d71a
thiselt.exe

42784

895

In order to carry out these instructions, you will need to write down or print all of the files and entries associated with the spyware. Then, you will turn on the computer in safe mode and manually remove all of the spyware files and entries. Since the list is so long, this will obviously be a tedious task. That is why it is best to wait until you have tried several types of antispyware software before manual removal.

It is also good to read some of the user comments which are generally posted after spyware removal instructions. This will give you an idea of what problems people are coming up against. And yes – there will almost always be some sort of problem!

Warning about Manual Spyware Removal

Keep in mind that you should always back up your PC before you attempt to remove any spyware or make any changes. It is very easy to remove the wrong files because spyware is often designed to mirror files which should be on a normally-functioning computer.

If you are not familiar with your computer's functions, it is best that you leave it to the professionals to remove spyware. There is too much of a risk that you could end up accidentally deleting an important file or entries and thus completely impairing your best to wait until you have tried several types of antispyware software before manual removal.

It is also good to read some of the user comments which are generally posted after spyware removal instructions. This will give you an idea of what problems people are coming up against. And yes – there will almost always be some sort of problem!

Warning about Manual Spyware Removal

Keep in mind that you should always back up your PC before you attempt to remove any spyware or make any changes. It is very easy to remove the wrong files because spyware is often designed to mirror files which should be on a normally-functioning computer.

If you are not familiar with your computer's functions, it is best that you leave it to the professionals to remove spyware. There is too much of a risk that you could end up accidentally deleting an important file or entries and thus completely impairing your computer's ability to function. One option is to hire a professional to teach you how to remove certain files and make sure that they are really deleted.

Even though this seems like a really futile cycle, there isn't much that regular internet users can do about it. As a new spyware is created, a specialized utility for combating the spyware is released. Then, the spyware creators seek holes in that new utility and exploit them for the next strain of spyware.

Chapter 16
Manual Spyware Removal without Instructions

When you have the name of the spyware which your computer is infected with, it is easy to find instructions for the spyware's removal. All you need to do is type in the spyware's name and you will get detailed instructions and users' comments to guide you through the process.

However, in order to get the name of the spyware, your antispyware needs to be able to detect it. Some spyware are so well hidden that your antispyware may not be able to find remove certain files and make sure that they are really deleted.

Even though this seems like a really futile cycle, there isn't much that regular internet users can do about it. As a new spyware is created, a specialized utility for combating the spyware is released. Then, the spyware creators seek holes in that new utility and exploit them for the next strain of spyware.

Chapter 16
Manual Spyware Removal without Instructions

When you have the name of the spyware which your computer is infected with, it is easy to find instructions for the spyware's removal. All you need to do is type in the spyware's name and you will get detailed instructions and users' comments to guide you through the process.

However, in order to get the name of the spyware, your antispyware needs to be able to detect it. Some spyware are so well hidden that your antispyware may not be able to find it at all. Also, if you don't have any antispyware and become infected, the spyware may not allow you to use antispyware. In this situation, you also won't be able to find the name of the spyware and look up its removal instructions online. Manual spyware removal is still possible in safe mode. However, you will have to find out where the spyware is located on your own.

There are seemingly millions of places where spyware can hide in your computer's system. Luckily, finding out where the spyware is hiding is not as hard as it used to be in the past.

First, you will want to start your computer in safe mode. Once in safe mode, press CTRL+ALT+Delete. The Task Manager will come up. Then, click on the processes tab. You will see a list of all of the processes which are essential to the Windows operating system. Make a list of all of these processes.

Next, restart your computer so you boot Windows normally. Then, look at the processes in Task Manager again. Make a list of these processes and compare it to your first list.

The second list from when Windows was booted normally should be longer than the first. From the second list, cross off any processes which were running in safe mode. Then cross of any processes which you may recognize.

What are left on the list are higher-level Windows processes, ad-on applications, spyware and any other infection your computer may have.

Now, you will need to go to www.processlibrary.com. At this site, you will be able to type in the name of the processes in order to find out what they are. This will keep you from deleting any potential vital processes from your computer. Process Library is good at keeping the list of processes updated so you should be able to find everything on your list. Any unidentified processes are likely spyware.

After finding out which of the processes are likely to be spyware, you should download a utility called StartupList. This utility can be used to show you which programs are launching when you boot Windows. This information will further help you identify any spyware on your computer as well as viruses or worms. You can find the utility here: http://www.spywareinfo.com/~merijn/downloads.html.

You should now have a list of all of the spyware files and entries. Then, you can go through your computer in safe mode and delete them all. This can be a very tedious procedure which is just made worse if you try to rush. Take your time to make sure that you remove all of the illicit files and entries.

Chapter 17
Combating Browser Hijackers

It seems like almost all new spyware software programs are now browser hijackers. These types of spyware will change your browser start page, search page, and/or favorite settings. The reason that this is done is to get extra traffic for the sites of certain websites. Since websites depend on traffic for success, browser hijacking is becoming a very large problem.

or worms. You can find the utility here:
http://www.spywareinfo.com/~merijn/downl
oads.html.

You should now have a list of all of the
spyware files and entries. Then, you can go
through your computer in safe mode and
delete them all. This can be a very tedious
procedure which is just made worse if you try
to rush. Take your time to make sure that you
remove all of the illicit files and entries.

Chapter 17
Combating Browser Hijackers

It seems like almost all new spyware software
programs are now browser hijackers. These
types of spyware will change your browser
start page, search page, and/or favorite
settings. The reason that this is done is to get
extra traffic for the sites of certain websites.
Since websites depend on traffic for success,
browser hijacking is becoming a very large
problem.

In some cases, you can return your browser
setting back to normal with just a few clicks of
the mouse.

In Internet Explorer, click on the Tools heading. Then click on Internet Options. Under the general tab, you will find a place to type in what you want to be your home page when your web browser starts up.

You will need to reset the search page. Do this by clicking on the Menu tab called Programs. Then, click on the button labeled as Reset Settings. You will get a prompt asking if you want to proceed. There is a box in the right-hand corner that says Reset Start Page. By clicking on this box before proceeding, you can reset your settings.

Open up the Favorites section in Internet Explorer. Delete all the spyware bookmarks.

Unfortunately, not all browser hijackers are this easy to fix. If the settings keep on going back to the spyware hijacked settings, then you will have to change it in the registry following these steps.

Click the Start button on your computer and then select Run. Type in the command regedit and then hit enter.

Your registry editor will appear. You need to find the Start Page which will be located in this path:

HKEY_CURRENT_USER\Software\Microsoft\Internet Explorer\Main

Double click on the Start Page entry. You will be able to enter the startup page that you want.

Now, you will need to reset your search pages. They are located in the same area as the registry editor and are labeled as such:

Search Page

Search Bar

Fill in the entries for the Search Page and Search Bar.

You will also need to check these paths and make sure that they are set to the right search engine:

HKEY_CURRENT_USER\Software\Microsoft\Internet Explorer\SearchURL

www.ingramcontent.com/pod-product-compliance
Lightning Source LLC
LaVergne TN
LVHW052311060326
832902LV00021B/3825